SINK OR SWIM

AFRICAN-AMERICAN LIFESAVERS
OF THE OUTER BANKS

A Publication in the Carolina Young People Series

SINK OR SWIM

AFRICAN-AMERICAN LIFESAVERS
OF THE OUTER BANKS

Carole Boston Weatherford

Coastal Carolina Press • *Wilmington, North Carolina*

For Caresse and Jeffery:

You are the wind in my sails.

Book and cover design by Kachergis Book Design
Cover art by James Melvin

LIBRARY OF CONGRESS CATALOGING-IN-PUBLICATION DATA

Weatherford, Carole Boston, 1956–
    Sink or swim : African-American lifesavers of the Outer Banks /
Carole Boston Weatherford.
        p.   cm.
    Includes bibliographical references (p. 77).
    Summary: Tells the story of the U.S. Lifesaving Service, which
was the precursor of the Coast Guard, and its only all black crew,
operating off Pea Island on the North Carolina coast, led by
Richard Etheridge.
        ISBN 1-928556-01-9 cloth   ISBN 1-928556-03-5 paper
    1. Etheridge, Richard, 1942–1900 Juvenile literature.   2. Afro-
American lifeboat crew members—North Carolina—Pea Island
Biography Juvenile literature.   3. United States. Life-saving
Service—History Juvenile literature.   4. Lifesaving stations—North
Carolina—Pea Island—History Juvenile literature.   5. Pea Island
(N.C.)—History Juvenile literature.   [1. Etheridge, Richard, 1841–
1900.   2. United States.   Life-saving Service—History.   3. Afro-
Americans—History.   4. Pea Island (N.C.)—History.]   I. Title.
VK1430.A1W43   1999
363.28'6—dc21   99-30125

The paper in this book meets the guidelines for permanence and dura-
bility of the Committee on Production Guidelines for Book Longevity
of the Council on Library Resources.

Coastal Carolina Press
University Place Office Park
4709 College Acres Drive, Suite 1
Wilmington, North Carolina 28403

CONTENTS

⟨decorative ornament⟩

ILLUSTRATIONS

ACKNOWLEDGMENTS

I extend thanks to Captain Steve Rochon for his cooperation and encouragement; to Katie and Pam Burkart for their enthusiasm and generosity; and to David Wright and David Zoby for the article that piqued my curiosity.

I received pictorial research assistance from the Outer Banks History Center, the North Carolina Aquarium at Roanoke Island, the U.S. Coast Guard Public Information Office, and the North Carolina Collection at the University of North Carolina–Chapel Hill Library.

I owe a debt of gratitude to my husband Ronald and children Caresse and Jeffery, who accompanied me to the Outer Banks to conduct primary research. Last but not least, I express appreciation to Kim Byerly, a Salem College student intern who helped with research.

SINK OR SWIM

AFRICAN-AMERICAN LIFESAVERS

OF THE OUTER BANKS

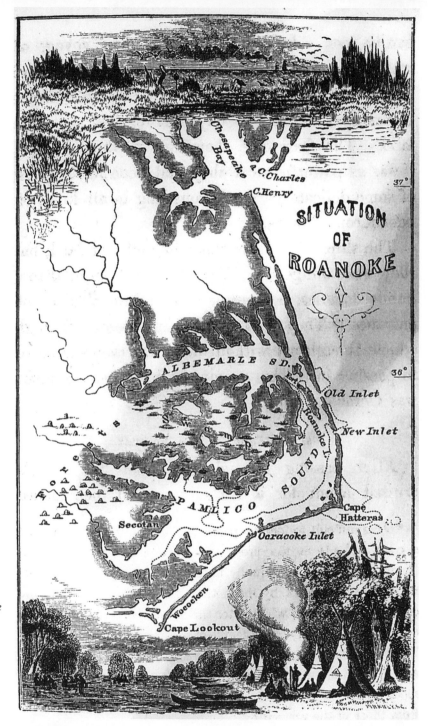

Roanoke Island map, 1860

INTRODUCTION

—⟨⟨⟨⟨⟩⟩⟩⟩—

THE OUTER BANKS, a slender chain of barrier islands, protect North Carolina's mainland by blocking angry waves and raging storms. Over thousands of years, wind, waves and weather formed the Outer Banks.

Long inhabited by Native Americans, the Outer Banks were in 1587 the first North American land that English explorers set foot upon. By 1590, however, the first English settlement had mysteriously disappeared, resulting in its being dubbed "The Lost Colony." During colonial times, the Outer Banks' inlets, narrow waterways between islands, were busy with trade between the colonies and England. The trade attracted pirates, such as Blackbeard, who hid on the Outer Banks and stole valuable cargo from ships.

As the Outer Banks became a central shipping route, concern grew about shipwrecks caused by shoals—sand bars in shallow water. So many ships sank off North Carolina's coast that statesman Alexander Hamilton called the waters the "Graveyard of the Atlantic." In 1794, the U.S. government authorized the first lighthouses along the Outer Banks—one at Shell Castle Island and another at Cape Hatteras—to warn ships of danger. At 180 feet, Cape Hatteras is the world's tallest brick lighthouse and one of ten dotting North Carolina's coastline.

Though lighthouses were built to prevent shipwrecks, many ships still ran aground. In 1871, the federal government established the U.S. Lifesaving Service, the forerunner of the U.S. Coast Guard, to rescue shipwreck victims. Lifesavers braved wind and waves to save lives. Along the North Carolina coast, the Pea Island U.S. Lifesaving Station had the service's only all-black crew. Under the leadership of Keeper Richard Etheridge, the Pea Island crew fought fierce waves and racial prejudice. In 1896, the crew even swam to a wreck during a hurricane, but the courageous lifesavers never received the recognition they deserved. A century later, the Pea Island crew was all but forgotten—until an eighth grader, a Coast Guard officer and two graduate students took up their cause. This is the story of the heroic Pea Island lifesavers.

CHAPTER 1

THE OCEAN REMEMBERS

Michael, row the boat ashore, Hallelujah!
Michael, row the boat ashore, Hallelujah!

Brother lend a helping hand, Hallelujah!
Brother lend a helping hand, Hallelujah!

Jordan's River is chilly cold, Hallelujah!
Kills the body but not the soul, Hallelujah!

—African-American spiritual

The loss of the Federal ironclad Monitor *in a storm, 1862*

THE WATERS off North Carolina's Outer Banks are known as the Graveyard of the Atlantic. Countless ships have been lost and thousands of seafarers have met their deaths here. The steamer *Home* sank near Ocracoke Island in 1837, leaving ninety dead. The next year, 100 died in the wreck of the steamer *Pulaski.* Twenty-three died in the wreck of the *Istria* in 1868. Nineteen perished in the wreck of the steamer *Strathairly* in 1891, and twenty-one in the wreck of the steamer *Ariosto* in 1899. Even the mighty *Monitor,* an iron battleship that won a historic victory in the Civil War, sank in a storm off the coast.

The list of lost vessels and lost lives is too long to recall. But the ocean remembers. Sometimes at low tide, ship skeletons poke through the sea's surface, sending haunting messages from the deep.

The ocean not only claimed lives—it also bred heroes. One was Richard Etheridge. In 1842, the same year a hurricane wrecked forty ships, he was born, on Roanoke Island, North Carolina, to Rachel Dough, a slave in the household of John Etheridge. A farmer and waterman, Etheridge taught Richard

The Affecting Situation of Mr. Cromie and his Family. — Page 76.

Survivors of the shipwrecked steamer Home, *1837*

Bald eagle

and his brother to read and write even though laws forbade teaching slaves.

Richard also learned about the sea. He fished the inlets and swam the surf. He watched snow geese nibble wild peas, and falcons and eagles soar above the dunes. He saw loggerhead turtles lay their eggs in the warm sands and watched hatchlings slowly thrash their way from nests to the water's edge. Richard loved the calm sound of water lapping at the shore.

But he knew the sea could also be cruel. As a young man, he performed rescues on his own. He braved the ocean's fury time and time again in his small fishing boat, knowing the sea could be friend or foe.

Loggerhead turtle

Wreck of the Priscilla, *1899*

CHAPTER 2

A CALL TO ARMS

Wade in the water, Wade in the water, children,
Wade in the water, God's gonna trouble the water.
O, Wade in the water, Wade in the water, children,
Wade in the water, God's gonna trouble the water.

—African-American spiritual

Charge of the Hawkins-Zouaves on Roanoke Island

T HE OCEAN was meek compared to the Civil War that pitted North against South and spilled blood on the land. After the Civil War broke out in 1861, waterways of the Outer Banks became important military targets. Nine Confederate forts defended the North Carolina coast. By the fall of 1861, however, Union troops controlled most of the Outer Banks.

In February 1862, General Ambrose Burnside, a Union commander, led more than 11,500 troops in defeating Confederate forces on Roanoke Island. The island became a Union stronghold and a refugee camp for more than 1,000 freed and es-

Union troops attack Roanoke Island

Distribution of clothing to ex-slaves in New Bern, 1862

caped slaves—known as freedmen. The African-American men served as porters for Union officers and soldiers and worked as cooks, teamsters, and woodcutters. Some were paid $8 per month plus rations and clothing to build Fort Burnside at the north end of Roanoke Island. Three-fourths of the freedmen were women and children, whom the government paid $4 per month and provided clothing, food, and supplies.

In 1863, the federal government established an official Freedman's Colony on Roanoke Island. The village included more than 600 houses, a school, store, hospital, and small church. The federal government also set up a steam mill, sawmill, and gristmill for the ex-slaves to run. In addition, the government granted to former slaves the lands that were abandoned by or confiscated from Confederate landowners.

When Union forces began accepting African Americans, some freedmen went to New Bern (then occupied by Union forces) to enlist in the army. Richard Etheridge joined the Thirty-Sixth United States Colored Troops, the Second North Carolina Colored Infantry. From South Carolina to Maryland, the Thirty-Sixth participated in Union operations, scout runs, and expeditions. The troops spent much of their first year of active duty guarding the Point Lookout,

African Americans enlist in U.S. Colored Troops

U.S. Colored Troops at Dutch Gap, Virginia

Maryland, prison camp and raiding nearby Virginia communities for freed or escaped slaves—contraband, as the Union forces called them.

The African-American troops finally had their moment of glory in the September 29, 1864 Battle of Chaffin's Farm. They helped overrun General Robert E. Lee's position at New Market Heights, Virginia. This important victory led to the defeat of Richmond, the Confederate capital. Twenty-one men of the Thirty-Sixth were killed, eighty-seven were wounded, and two received Congressional Medals of Honor for bravery. Two days after the battle, Richard Etheridge was promoted to the rank of sergeant.

CHAPTER 3

FIGHTING FOR JUSTICE

I am on the battlefield for my Lord,
I'm on the battlefield for my Lord;
And I promised him that I would serve
    him till I die.
I'm on the battlefield for my Lord.

        —African-American spiritual

Union soldiers stealing pigs, 1862

R ICHARD ETHERIDGE fought not only for freedom on the battlefield. He also fought for fair treatment of the ex-slaves living in Union Army camps on Roanoke Island. With William Benson, a fellow soldier, Etheridge wrote a letter to General O. O. Howard, commissioner of the Freedmen's Bureau, a government agency formed to help ex-slaves and poor whites. The letter accused white Union soldiers of breaking into blacks' homes, stealing food, and punishing blacks who fought back. The letter was not merely a complaint—it was an appeal for protection for the ex-slaves.

The 1865 letter read:

Genl We the soldiers of the 36 U.S. Col Regt Humbly petition to you to alter the Affairs at Roanoke Island. We have served in the US Army faithfully and don our duty to our Country, for which we thank God (that we had the opportunity) but at the same time our family's are suffering at Roanoke Island N.C.

When we were enlisted in the service we were prommised that our wifes and family's should receive rations from goverment. The rations for our wifes and family's have been (and are now cut down) to one half the regular ration. Consequently three or four days out of every ten days, thee have nothing to eat. at the same time our ration's are stolen from the ration house by Mr Streeter the Asst Supt at the Island (and others) and sold while our family's are suffering for some thing to eat.

Mr Streeter the Asst Supt of Negro aff's at Roanoke Island is a througher Cooper head a man who says that he is no part of a Abolitionist. takes no care of the colored people and has no Simpathy with the colored people. A man who kicks our wives and children out of the ration house or commissary, he takes no notice of their actual suffering and sells the rations and allows it to be sold, and our family's suffer for something to eat.

Captn James the Suptn in Charge has been told of these facts and has taken no notice of them. so has Coln Lahaman the Commander in Charge of Roanoke, but no notice is taken of it, because it comes from Contrabands or Freedmen the cause of much suffering is that Captn James has not paid the Colored people for their work for near a year and at the same time cuts the ration's off to one half so the people have neither provisions or money to buy it with. There are men on the Island that have been wounded at Dutch Gap Canal, working there, and some discharged soldiers, men that were wounded in the service of the U.S. Army, and returned home to Roanoke that Cannot get any rations and are not able to work, some soldiers are sick in Hospitals that have never been paid a cent and their familys are suffering and their children going crying without anything to eat.

our familys have no protection the white soldiers break into our houses act as they please steal our chickens rob our gardens and if any one defends their-Selves against them they are taken to the gard house for it. so our familys have no protection when Mr Streeter is here to protect them and will not do it.

Genl we the soldiers of the 36 U.S. Co Troops having familys at Roanoke Island humbly petition you to favour us by removeing Mr Streeter the present Asst Supt at Roanoke Island under Captn James.

Genl prehaps you think the Statements against Mr Streeter too strong, but we can prove them.

Genl order Chaplain Green to Washington to report the true state of things at Roanoke Island. Chaplain Green is an asst Supt at Roanoke Island, with Mr Holland Streeter and he can prove the facts. and there are plenty of white men here that can prove them also, and many more thing's not mentioned.

Richard Etheridge and William Benson closed their strongly worded protest, "Signed in behalf of humanity."

Other soldiers and freedmen also complained, and Assistant Superintendent Streeter was eventually punished. He was replaced by S. H. Birdsall.

When the Civil War ended, Etheridge's unit was sent to Texas to fight in the Indian Wars and Mexican border conflicts. The African-American soldiers were hardly treated as heroes. On the contrary, their pay went ten months overdue and their rations were cut in half. To make matters worse, their families on Roanoke Island continued to suffer abuse at the hands of Union troops. In 1865 when the African-American troops were being reorganized into the Buffalo Soldiers, Etheridge was discharged from the Army. His military training, however, stuck with him throughout his life.

CHAPTER 4

SURFMAN NO. 6

Go tell all my friends
That my ship just came sailin' in
It came filled with the Holy Ghost
Filled with joy divine
Wouldn't you like to sail on a ship like mine
Get on board, get on board, get on board

—African-American work song

Camp meeting at Roanoke Island church

R ICHARD ETHERIDGE returned to Roanoke Island with his wife, Frances, and daughter, Lurena. Federal forces moved many of the former slaves off the Outer Banks after the Freedmen's Colony was abandoned in 1866. Some, like Etheridge, remained on Roanoke Island.

To support his family, Richard worked as a fisherman. He knew the salty waters and sandy shores

Herring being pulled from nets, 1879

like the back of his hand. That knowledge would be important in the Lifesaving Service.

The U.S. Lifesaving Service was founded in 1871 to rescue shipwreck victims. In 1874, North Carolina had seven lifesaving stations, some thirty miles apart. Etheridge joined the Lifesaving Service in 1875 as Surfman No. 6 at the Oregon Inlet station.

Each station had a keeper or commander and six surfmen, who carried out rescues. Surfmen had to be strong swimmers and able to handle heavy equipment. Most black lifesavers held the lowest rank, Surfman No. 6. They usually worked as stations' cooks and stable hands and rarely as surfmen.

Keepers decided which rescue method and equipment to use. When the wreck was near the beach and the surf was too violent to row out in a surfboat, the crew used the beach apparatus to

Dragging the beach apparatus cart

26

bring victims ashore. Before the Lifesaving Service provided horses and mules for hauling, the surfmen dragged the heavy beach apparatus cart, sometimes for several miles, through the soft wet sand to the spot on shore closest to the stranded vessel.

On the beach, the crew unloaded and then assembled the rescue equipment. Two surfmen set and charged a small cannon to fire a shot line, a light rope, out to the wreck. The wooden faking box, which looked like an oversized weaving loom, kept the shot line untangled as it uncoiled. One loop of a coil was referred to as a fake. Shot lines could be up to 800 yards long.

Faking box with coiled lines

Two other surfmen assembled and buried the sand anchor and erected the crotch, an X-shaped wood frame. The wooden sand anchor held a double pulley and steadied the ten-foot crotch that propped the line above the surf to prevent victims from drowning while being pulled ashore.

Battling wind, rain, snow, fog, darkness, and distance, the keeper fired the cannon to send the shot line to the wreck. He aimed for the rigging, the ropes that supported and worked the ship's masts, yards, and sails. A lead weight on the end of the shot line helped propel it through the wind. Sometimes, several shots were required to reach the wreck. Connected to the shot line was a large pulley (called a tail block) threaded with a whip. The whip was an endless line forming a continuous loop. A tally board, a wooden tablet with instructions in English and French, was tied to the endless line. The tally board told victims how to use the lifesaving equipment and to land women and children first.

On the wreck, the victims attached the pulley to a stable part of the ship, such as the mast. On the shore, the surfmen tied a heavy rope (called a hawser) on the endless line and drew the rope to the wreck using the pulley. The victims tied the heavy rope to the ship two feet above the pulley. The surfmen tied their end of the rope to the sand anchor's double pulley, then pulled the rope taut.

The breeches buoy, a pair of canvas shorts sewn around a life preserver ring, hung from the heavy

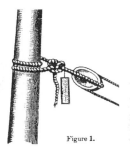

Figure 1.

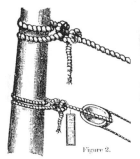

Figure 2.

An endless line, pulley, and heavy rope tied to the ship's mast for a rescue

rope by another pulley and four ropes. Using pulleys, the surfmen sent the breeches buoy or life car out to the wreck. The breeches buoy consisted of canvas shorts sewn to a lifesaving ring and hung on a thick rope. One at a time, victims sat in the breeches buoy and fastened its suspenders. Then, the surfmen tugged them ashore. Dangling over the ocean, head barely above the swirling sea, the victim in the breeches buoy inched toward safety. Children were tied into the buoy or held by older victims. If two victims each put one leg through the breeches buoy, the surfmen could save two people at once.

Occasionally, the crew sent a life car instead of the breeches buoy. The metal life car looked like a covered boat and held four to six people. In an enclosed compartment, the life car protected survivors from fierce waves as the surfmen pulled it across the water. As with all rescues, the surfmen had to work fast. There was limited breathable air inside the life car. Also, the life car was extremely heavy and strained the rope.

Victim in a breeches buoy

In 1878 the Lyle gun, a 150-pound cannon invented by Army Lieutenant David A. Lyle, replaced heavier cannons. The Lyle gun could fire a shot line up to 695 yards—farther than older cannons.

Life car

Beach rescues were not possible when the beach was flooded or when wrecks were too far from shore to be reached by a shot line. In such cases, the crew used the thirty-four foot wooden surfboat to perform rescues. The surfboat (also known as a life-boat) held ten to twelve passengers.

Lyle gun

Before horses were employed, the crewmen pulled the boat on its four-wheel carriage to the scene of the wreck. After unloading the boat, the surfmen waded out with the craft to get it beyond the breakers. A few surfmen steadied the boat while others scrambled aboard. Then, they began the backbreaking and life-threatening trip to the wreck. The keeper steered while the crew pulled the oars. Sometimes they rowed for hours, several miles through merciless waves, turbulent winds, and driving rain, to bring victims to safety ashore.

The breeches buoy and life car may appear peculiar, but they saved many lives. In fact, these methods were used until helicopters replaced them in the 1950s.

When not in use, rescue equipment was stored at the lifesaving station. Each station was a two-story house topped with an open watchtower. The station also had a stable and corral for mules or horses. The station's first floor had an eating and living area and a large boat room. The second floor had three rooms: a storage area; cramped sleeping quarters for the crew and shipwreck victims; and

A crew launches a lifeboat.

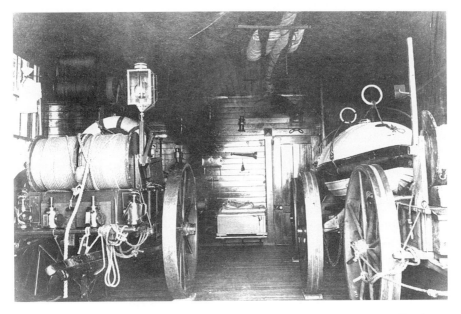

Beach apparatus cart and life car in a station's boat room

private quarters for the keeper. During active season, originally from December through March, crews lived at the stations.

Keepers earned $400 a year, a good sum at a time when many people on the Outer Banks were poor. Government jobs offered the highest pay around, and dishonest public officials gave lifesaving jobs to their friends and relatives. Some keepers and crewmen were unskilled and unfit.

This situation caused many deaths. During the winter of 1877–78, 188 victims and surfmen died in shipwrecks off the Outer Banks. In November 1877,

Collecting bodies from the Metropolis *disaster, 1878*

the U.S. warship *Huron* ran aground less than three miles from the Nags Head Station, which was padlocked for the eight-month off-season. Ninety-eight people lost their lives. During the January 1878 wreck of the steamer *Metropolis,* mistakes by the Jones Hill Station's crew left eighty-five dead. The mounting death toll prompted Congress to lengthen the service's active season from four months to eight—September 1 to May 1—and to authorize the

U.S.L.S.S.

Stations

on the Outer Banks

Deals Island (Wash Woods), 1878

Old Currituck Inlet (Pennys Hill), 1878

Jones Hill (Whales Head/Currituck Beach), 1874

Poyners Hill, 1878

Caffeys Inlet, 1874

Paul Gamiels Hill, 1878

Kitty Hawk, 1874

Kill Devil Hills, 1878

Nags Head, 1874

Tommys Hummock (Bodie Island), 1878

Bodie Island (Oregon Inlet), 1874

Pea Island, 1878

New Inlet, 1882

Chicamacomico, 1874

Cedar Hummock (Gull Shoal), 1878

Little Kinnakeet, 1874

Big Kinnakeet, 1878

Cape Hatteras, 1880

Hatteras (Durants), 1878

Ocracoke (Hatteras Inlet), 1883

Creeds Hill, 1878

Ocracoke, 1904

Portsmouth, 1894

U.S. Lifesaving Stations on the North Carolina coast,
1874–1904

35

construction of eleven more lifesaving stations in North Carolina, including one at Pea Island. The U.S. Lifesaving Service also added a seventh surfman to each station's crew.

Lifesaving crews still made grave mistakes. Seven lives were lost in the 1879 wreck of the schooner *M&E Henderson.* That night, keeper George Daniels and some surfmen had left the Pea Island station unmanned to hunt waterfowl. Another surfman had also skipped the night patrol. Even worse, Keeper Daniels falsely reported having done a rescue that he did not perform. Charles Shoemaker, a Northern inspector for the U.S. Lifesaving Service, suggested firing Daniels and two surfmen and moving the rest of the crew to other stations.

Inspector Shoemaker had to fill the vacancies at Pea Island, but first he had to appoint a new keeper. With that appointment, Shoemaker took a bold step. "I recommend Richard Etheridge, colored, now No. 6 surfman in Station No. 16," the inspector wrote. "I examined this man, and found him to be thirty-eight years of age, strong robust physique, intelligent, and able to keep the Journal of the station. He is reported one of the best surfmen on this part of the coast of North Carolina."

Shoemaker continued, "I am aware that no col-

ored man holds the position of keeper in the Life-saving Service, and yet such as are surfmen, are found to be the best on the coast of North Carolina. I have given this matter as careful consideration as I am capable of, and have tried to weigh every argument, for and against its adoption, and I am fully convinced that the efficiency of the service at this station, will be greatly advanced by the appointment of this man to the Keepership of Station No. 17."

Inspector Frank Newcomb added, "Richard

Storm off Cape Hatteras, 1853

Etheridge . . . [is] as good a surfman as there is on the coast, black or white."

Etheridge's qualifications were well known. But the appointment of an African-American keeper represented uncharted waters. Racial attitudes were hardening in the South, and legalized segregation, known as Jim Crow, had begun to take hold. The new keeper would have his work cut out for him.

CHAPTER 5

THE PEA ISLAND STATION

—⬤—

When the storms of life are raging,
Stand by me;
When the storms of life are raging,
Stand by me.
When the world is tossing me,
Like a ship upon the sea;
Thou who rulest wind and water,
Stand by me.

> —*from "Stand by Me"*
> *Charles Albert Tindley (1851–1933)*

Pea Island Keeper Richard Etheridge (left) *led the U.S. Lifesaving Service's only all-black crew.*

I N 1880, Richard Etheridge became the first black keeper in the U.S. Lifesaving Service. But the shake-up at Pea Island merely began with his promotion. Unwilling to take orders from a black man, the station's four white surfmen quit. Two black surfmen, William Davis and William Daniel, stayed on. Two black surfmen, Lewis Wescott and William Bowser, were transferred from other stations. Two Roanoke Island watermen, Henry Daniel and George Midgett, rounded out the first all-black crew.

Local whites, hoping to cause the black lifesavers to quit, trumped up a rumor that blacks' jobs in the service were threatened. White townspeople claimed that Etheridge's transfer was part of a plan to isolate and then get rid of the black lifesavers. But the scare tactics didn't work; the black surfmen stayed on.

Stressing readiness, Etheridge drove the surfmen as if they were soldiers. To build their strength, he unhitched the mules from the heavy surfboat and had the crew drag the boat through the sand by hand. Each day was set aside for a different duty. The crew cleaned the station and repaired and polished equipment on Tuesdays. On Wednesdays they practiced signal flags, and on Thursdays they drilled with the beach apparatus and breeches buoys. They devoted Fridays to practicing first aid and resuscitation methods and Saturdays to laundry and personal gear. Sundays were set aside for rest and worship. The surfmen had rotating days off each week. For example, a surfman would be off on Monday one week, Tuesday the next week, Wednesday the next, and so on. Days off were the only time surfmen could see their families on the mainland.

Besides endless drills, Etheridge taught the

Dragging the lifeboat

Firing a line

surfmen to read and write so they could pass the civil service examination required of government employees.

Most importantly, the crew kept watch for boats in trouble. On clear days, a lookout in the station's tower noted passing ships and sent warnings with signal flags. At night and on foggy or stormy days, two lookouts toting lanterns and signal flares patrolled the beach. They walked in opposite directions—north and south—halfway to the neighboring stations. At the halfway point each Pea Island lookout exchanged a token with a lookout from a neighboring station. This proved that the lookouts had completed their patrols.

A surfman signals a ship

A surfman patrols the beach

The keeper steers the surfboat

As keeper, Etheridge kept a daily log, wrote
monthly reports, and led all rescues. He chose the
rescue method, and he took the steering oar on the
surfboat. He believed in the service's unofficial
motto: "The book says you have to go out and that's
a fact. Nothin' says you have to come back."

CHAPTER 6

TESTS OF COURAGE

I stood on de ribber ob Jerdon,
to see dat ship come sailin' ober;
stood on de ribber ob Jerdon,
to see dat ship sail by.
O moaner, don't ya weep,
when ya see dat ship come sailin' ober,
Shout "Glory, Hallelujah!"
When ya see dat ship sail by.

—African-American spiritual

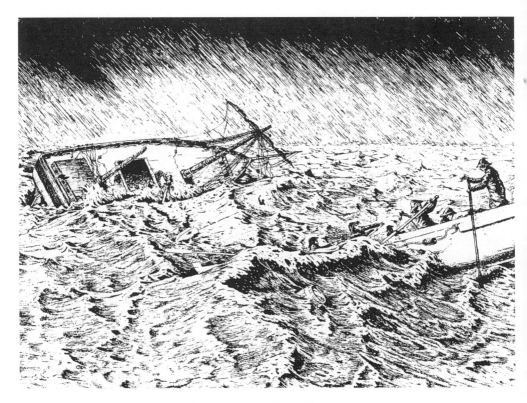

A crew performs a rescue with a surfboat

THE ALL-BLACK CREW survived their first season and returned to their families and other occupations. During off-season, however, disaster struck. On May 29, 1880, the Pea Island station caught fire and burned to the ground. Witnesses' testimonies hinted that three white surfmen from other stations had set the fire to scare off the black crew. The inspector, however, charged no one with the crime because he feared that arrests might fuel more racial hatred.

The next season, the Pea Island lifesavers worked out of the stables while building a new station. Etheridge made sure his crew obeyed orders to the letter, and Pea Island became known as one of the best-run stations in the area.

Few rescues went totally by the book. On October 5, 1881, Etheridge woke up sick. Early in the morning, a sharp Pea Island surfman spotted a grounded and wrecked schooner off the inlet. The Pea Island crew called off breakfast and joined the Chicamacomico Station crew in the rescue. Battling a high fever, Richard led his crew through howling winds to haul the boat trailer over sand and surf. By sundown, the two crews had failed to reach the scene and to rescue the thirteen people stranded on the wreck. In the meantime, three of the shipwreck victims jumped overboard and swam ashore. Four more died trying. Twenty-eight hours passed before six survivors from the schooner *Thomas J. Lancaster* were finally brought ashore.

The Pea Island crew assisted in many successful rescues, as this letter from the grateful crew of the schooner *Charles C. Lister, Jr.,* attests: "We came ashore in the morning of the 22nd [December 1888] in a heavy north-by-west gale, and we want to inform you of the timely heroic service that was rendered us by the crews of the Oregon Inlet and Pea Island Stations. They bravely did their work in saving our lives, landing everyone safe. . . . If they had not been on hand we should likely all have been lost."

The black lifesavers' most daring rescue occurred on October 11, 1896, during a storm which the *Wilmington Messenger* described as one of the heaviest in nearly half a century. On the way from Providence, Rhode Island, to Norfolk, Virginia, the schooner *E.S. Newman* lost its sails in a hurricane. Crashing waves sent the boat 100 miles off course

A surfman signals at night

and threatened to tear it apart. As the ship took in
sea water, Captain S. A. Gardiner decided to beach
the *Newman,* hoping to save his wife, his three-
year-old son Thomas, and his crew of six. The
schooner ran aground at around seven in the
evening, about two miles north of the Pea Island
station. The captain fired a flare and said a silent
prayer.

CHAPTER 7

A STORM RAGES

Master, the tempest is raging!
The billows are tossing high!
The sky is o'ershadowed with blackness,
No shelter or help is nigh:
"Carest Thou not that we perish?
How canst Thou lie asleep,
When each moment so madly is threat'ning
A grave in the angry deep?

—from "Peace Be Still!"
Mary A. Baker

A crew on the way to a wreck

E THERIDGE had stopped beach patrols during the storm, but surfman Theodore Meekins kept watch from the station's tower. Through heavy fog, driving rain, and blowing sand, Meekins thought he saw something. He lit a red Coston lamp, scanned the darkness, and saw nothing. But he couldn't be sure. Meekins signalled the keeper. The two lit another lamp. This time, the *Newman* answered with a flare.

Etheridge gathered his crew. With a pair of mules and a surfboat, the seven men headed for the wreck. "The storm was raging fearfully, the storm tide was sweeping across the beach, and the team was often brought to a standstill by the sweeping current," Etheridge later wrote. Knee-deep in sand and chilly water, the men pushed on. The swirling seas had flooded the coastline, leaving no firm ground where the crew could plant the sand anchor or place the Lyle gun to fire a lifeline. That ruled out a beach rescue. Nor could the men row the surfboat out to the wreck through the fierce waves.

So close to the wreck, yet so far. The *Newman*'s crew cheered when they spotted the lifesaving crew

[FORM 1808.]

JOURNAL.

Pea Island Station. District No. _Sixth_

Sunday, _Oct. 11th_, 189 _6_

CONDITION OF THE SURF.			
MIDNIGHT.	SUNRISE.	NOON.	SUNSET.
Smooth	Smooth	Smooth	Smooth
Light	Light	Light	Light
Moderate	Moderate	Moderate	Moderate
Strong	Strong	Strong	Strong
Rough	Rough	Rough	Rough
High	High	High	High
Very high X	Very high X	Very high X	Very high X

☞ The keeper will make a cross immediately after the word indicating the condition of the surf at midnight, sunrise, noon, and sunset.

Direction and force of wind, and state of weather at midnight,
Fresh N.E. gale Stormy

Direction and force of wind, and state of weather at sunrise,
Fresh N.E. gale Stormy

Direction and force of wind, and state of weather at noon,
Fresh N. Hurricane Stormy

Direction and force of wind, and state of weather at sunset,
Fresh N. Hurricane Stormy

ENTER THE READING OF BAROMETER AND THERMOMETER AT MIDNIGHT, SUNRISE, NOON, AND SUNSET.

Barometer—Midnight, _30—2_ ; Sunrise, _30_ ; Noon, _30—_ ; Sunset, _30—1_

Thermometer—Midnight, _65_ ; Sunrise, _65_ ; Noon, _62_ ; Sunset, _60_

(Fill in, in the blank spaces below, the names of the patrolmen or watch, the names of the patrolmen met, and the name of the station the latter were from.)

PATROL.

W. H. Irving, No. 6, midnight to 3 a. m., met _C. S. Hassomen, No. 1 from Oreg on Inlet_ Station.

B. W. Wise, No. 1, midnight to 3 a. m., met _Stoped at New Inlet at 40 m past 1 a.m._

B. L. Bowsin, No. 1, 3 a. m. to sunrise, met _Rp. S. Midgett, No. 2, Oreg on Inlet_

L. L. Wescott, No. 2, 3 a. m. to sunrise, met _Stoped at New Inlet depot 4 a.m._

L. L. Pugh No. 3, sunset to 9 p. m., met   "

Thos. Meekins No. 4, sunset to 9 p. m., met   "

W. Wise No. 5, 9 p. m. to midnight, met   "

W. H. Irving No. 6, 9 p. m. to midnight, met   "

Is the house thoroughly clean? _Yes_

Is the house in good repair? _Yes Yes_

Is the apparatus in good condition? _Yes Yes_

How many members of the crew (including Keeper) were present? _7_

Who were absent, and why?

Name of substitute: in place of   surfman.

(Fill in the number of vessels of each class that have passed the Station this day.)

Ships,   barks,   brigs,   schooners,   steamers,   sloops,

GENERAL REMARKS.

(Under this head are to be stated all transactions relating to house or service.)

The patrolman on watch from sunset to 9 P.M. discovered from the station Brow through the blinding storm. a distress signal to the south of the station. which was immediately answered with a coston signal and informed the keeper of the fact, who burned a red rocket which was answered again with a red torch light then it became an evident fact that some vessel was stranded on the beach, although the storm and hurricane which the weather bureau had given notice of on the 10 inst., was raging fearfully and the sea tide was sweeping a cross the beach so fearfully that no patroling could be done but the keeper at once mustered the crew and with the team a pair of good mules started to the scene of disaster with the hand car and driving cart. although it seemed impossible under such unfavorable circumstances to render any assistance, the team was often brought to a standstill by the sweeping current in the distance. The lifesavers heard the cries of the captain's wife and child.

Although there was little hope for a rescue, the lifesavers at least had to try. Etheridge came up with a plan. He called his two strongest surfmen and gave the order, "Tie a large sized shot line around [them] . . . and send them down through the surf as near the side of the vessel as possible."

Tied with heavy rope and lugging an extra line, the two surfmen waded and swam through churning foam toward the battered boat. The crewmen onshore gripped the other end of the rope. The swimmers often disappeared in the roaring waves. When the surfmen neared the boat, they threw the end of the lifeline on board. Then, they climbed the ladder lowered by the ship's crew.

The *Newman*'s crew lashed the captain's son to the surfmen with another line. As waves beat the schooner, the surfmen struggled back to shore. The six surfmen took turns swimming in pairs to the shipwreck. In six hours, they carried all nine people, one by one, to safety. Later, the lifesavers and survivors huddled around a warm fire in the Lifesaving Station.

Richard Etheridge and his crew had fought the stormy sea and won. But, unlike white lifesavers who were honored for less heroic rescues, the Pea Island crew received no medals for risking their lives. All they got was the *E.S. Newman* nameboard, which Captain Gardiner gave them after finding it on the beach. Surfman Meekins nailed the nameboard to the side of his barn.

The crewmen became local legends. African-American boys on Roanoke Island dreamed of becoming lifesavers when they grew up.

Surfmen swim to the wreck of the E.S. Newman

Nameboard off the E.S. Newman

Richard Etheridge was keeper until his death in 1900. He is buried on the site of the current North Carolina Aquarium on Roanoke Island.

By 1904 the U.S. Lifesaving Service had placed the Pea Island station in a separate district, so white surfmen would not lose their eligibility for appointments by refusing posts there. Eventually, Pea Island was the only station in North Carolina where blacks were assigned and the only one where they could hope to become keeper. Benjamin Bowser succeeded Richard Etheridge as keeper, but died

Richard Etheridge's gravesite on the grounds of the North Carolina Aquarium on Roanoke Island

59

Lifesaver Herbert Collins in the Pea Island surfboat, c. 1940

after barely two months of service. Lewis Wescott became keeper on October 4, 1900.

In 1915, the U.S. Lifesaving Service became part of the U.S. Coast Guard. Except for a brief stint in the late 1930s by Palmer Midgett, a white keeper, the Pea Island crew remained all-black until the U.S. Coast Guard closed the station in 1947. Pea Island's last officer in charge was Chief Boatswain's Mate Maxie M. Berry, Sr.

Pea Island Station during World War II

Chief Boatswain's Mate Maxie Berry, Sr., Pea Island's last commanding officer

CHAPTER 8

FORGOTTEN HEROES

'Tis the old ship of Zion, 'tis the old ship of Zion,
'tis the old ship of Zion, get on board, get on
    board.

It has landed many a thousand, it has landed
    many a thousand,
it has landed many a thousand, get on board, get
    on board.

Ain't no danger in the water, ain't no danger in
    the water,
ain't no danger in the water, get on board, get on
    board.

It will take us all to heaven, it will take us all to
    heaven,
it will take us all to heaven, get on board, get on
    board.

—African-American spiritual

Signaling from the watchtower, c. 1940

Crew rolling the lifeboat trailer, c. 1940

I N T H E sixty-nine years that Pea Island Station operated, its crews received more inspection commendations and saved more lives—over 600—than any other station in the Lifesaving Service. William Simmons, who served at Pea Island during the 1920s, explained what drove the black crews: "We knew we were colored and . . . felt we had to do better whether anybody said so or not."

Decades later, the black lifesavers' story may as well have been buried on the ocean floor. Coast Guard Captain Stephen Rochon stumbled upon the rescuers' tale in a dusty, yellowed file while planning a 1988 Black History Month program. Fascinated by their story, Rochon began giving speeches about the crew.

Slowly but surely, the Pea Island crew gained broader recognition. In 1991, a granite memorial honoring the lifesavers was placed at Richard Etheridge's grave site on the grounds of the current North Carolina Aquarium at Roanoke Is-

Waving signal flags, c. 1940

Captain Stephen Rochon, U.S. Coast Guard

U.S. Coast Guard patrol boat Pea Island

land. The late Alex Haley, a retired Coast Guard officer and the author of *Roots*, spoke at the memorial dedication. ". . . I heard many, many times—dozens, scores of times—about the legendary Pea Island," he said. Also in 1991, a new patrol boat was put into service as the USCG *Pea Island*.

In 1993, Virginia Commonwealth University graduate writing students David Wright and David Zoby contacted Rochon

Pictured (left to right) are David Wright, Katie Burkart, and David Zoby

about the lifesavers. They all agreed that the U.S. Lifesaving Service had unjustly denied the crew medals. Rochon told Wright and Zoby, "We can set history straight."

The three men—two black and one white— joined forces to right a wrong. For two years they worked as if on a mission, with Wright and Zoby doing research and Rochon preparing a medal recommendation. Then in 1995, Rochon learned from the Coast Guard's Medals and Awards Branch that Katie Burkart, a white eighth grader from Washington, North Carolina, had written letters urging President Bill Clinton, Senator Jesse Helms, Congresswoman Eva Clayton, and other public officials to honor the Pea Island crew.

Katie wrote:

Dear President Clinton,

Enclosed you will find an essay I researched and wrote concerning Richard Etheridge and the life-saving crew at Pea Island Station, which was the only all black life-saving crew in the entire life-saving service. Throughout their service, the Pea Island crew never received any formal recognition for their heroic actions. For the rescue of the E.S. Newman alone, they should have received the Gold Life Saving Medal. . . .

I realize all the crew members are deceased. However, I would appreciate it greatly if you could arrange for some formal commemoration or honor to be bestowed upon their memories.

At this time in our state and nation, when young people, like myself, need role models, what better example than Richard Etheridge and his crew. Reconstruction was the worst of eras for our nation and state. However, during this turbulent and violent time, these men showed responsibility and honor by doing their best and beyond. Please help make these honorable and heroic men notable in not only North Carolina history, but nationally as well. None are more deserving.

Katie's letter sparked action. President Clinton wrote the Coast Guard commandant, and Senator Helms's office began a Congressional inquiry. Sensing that the time was right to push for a medal, Rochon finished and submitted his sixty-nine-page medal recommendation. In a letter that accompanied the recommendation, Rochon noted, "surviving family members of the Pea Island Lifesavers . . . have waited many years for their ancestors to be properly honored."

On October 31, 1995, the wait finally ended. Admiral Robert Kramek, the commandant of the U.S. Coast Guard, approved the awarding of the Gold Lifesaving Medal to the Pea Island Station.

*The Commandant of the United States Coast Guard
requests the pleasure of your company
at a ceremony to present
the Gold Lifesaving Medal (posthumously) to the crewmen
of U.S. Life-Saving Station Pea Island, North Carolina
on Tuesday, the fifth of March at half past ten o'clock
U.S. Navy Memorial, Washington, D.C.*

R.S.V.P.　　　　　　　　*Service Dress Blue*
(202) 267-1587　　　　　*or equivalent Civilian attire*

Invitation to U.S. Coast Guard gold medal ceremony

CHAPTER 9

GOLD MEDALS

⟨ornament⟩

Courage my soul, and let us journey on,
Tho' the night is dark it won't be very long.
Thanks be to God, the morning light appears,
And the storm is passing over, Hallelujah!

Soon we shall reach the distant shining shore,
Free from the storms we'll rest evermore.
Safe within the veil, we'll furl the riven sail,
And the storm is passing over, Hallelujah!

—from *"The Storm Is Passing Over"*
Charles Albert Tindley (1851–1933)

Descendants of the Pea Island lifesavers attend the medal ceremony: (left) *BMC Frank Hester, grandnephew of Dorman Pugh; and* (right) *William Bowser, former Pea Island lifesaver, cousin of Benjamin Bowser.*

O N MARCH 5, 1996, almost a century after the *Newman* rescue, the Pea Island lifesavers finally received their due. Katie, Rochon, Wright, Zoby, and descendants of the Pea Island lifesavers gathered at the Navy Memorial in Washington for the long-overdue medal ceremony.

Admiral Robert Kramek, commandant of the U.S. Coast Guard, unveiled the gold medal and read the award citation:

"For extreme and heroic daring on the evening of October 11, 1896, following the shipwreck of the schooner *E.S. Newman* in the Atlantic Ocean near Cape Fear, North Carolina. Keeper Richard Etheridge gallantly led his six brave surfmen through fierce hurricane winds and pounding waves. Arriving on scene in pitch darkness, with near zero visibility, Etheridge and his fearless crew . . . risked their lives as they waded and swam out to the wreck to extricate the battered passengers and crew from the vessel. Again and again, the Pea Island Station crew went back through the raging sea, literally carrying

Admiral Robert Kramek, commandant of the U.S. Coast Guard, awards the Gold Lifesaving Medal to the Pea Island Station crew.

all nine persons from certain death to the safety of the shore. The Pea Island Station crew, under great difficulties, tremendous personal risk, and imminent peril, performed a truly remarkable feat of heroism. Their unselfish actions and valiant service reflect the highest credit upon themselves and are in keeping with the highest traditions of humanitarian service."

Katie also spoke at the ceremony: "Richard Etheridge, Benjamin Bowser, Lewis Wescott, Dorman Pugh, Theodore Meekins, Stanley Wise, William Irving. I say these names out loud by way of atonement for the many years they have been lost to us."

"Kindness and courage," she concluded, "sooner or later find some recognition."

On that stormy night in 1896, no one cared about medals

or skin color. What mattered was that help arrived and lives were saved.

For the brave Pea Island crew, that was all in a day's work.

Gold Lifesaving Medal awarded to the Pea Island Station crew

Berlin, Ira; Reidy, Joseph; and Rowland, Leslie, eds. *The Black Military Experience,* Freedom: A Documentary History of Emancipation, 1861–1867, 2d ser. Cambridge, England: Cambridge University Press, 1982, 729–30.

Bowser, William. Author interview (via phone), August 14, 1998.

Burkart, Katie. Author interview (via phone), August 1998.

———. "Speech for the Pea Island Lifesaving Station Gold Lifesaving Medal Ceremony." March 5, 1996, Washington, DC, 1.

———. "Letter to President Bill Clinton." April 4, 1995, Washington, NC.

"Captain Richard Etheridge." United States Lifesaving Service, (February 23, 1972) Coast Guard News, Press Release No. 26–72.

Dunn, Gordon E., and Miller, Banner I. *Atlantic Hurricanes.* Baton Rouge, LA: Louisiana State University Press, 1960, 294.

Etheridge, Richard. "Pea Island Station Log." August 1, 1896–July 31, 1897. National Archives, East Point Branch, East Point, GA.

Glass, Jon. "Belated tribute: Memorial salutes black lifesaving post." *Virginian-Pilot and Ledger Star,* February 10, 1991, A1.

Mobley, Joe A. *Ship Ashore! The U.S. Lifesavers of Coastal North Carolina.* Raleigh, NC: North Carolina Division of Archives and History, 1995.

O'Brien, Michael, T. "Black Heroes of Pea Island." *Commandants Bulletin* (June 1980): 6.

Picker, Lester A. "Roots of black lifesaving team." *Baltimore Sun,* February 22, 1998, 2A.

Purdy, Gregory M. "The Life-Saving Station at Pea Island." April 28, 1992. Typescript.

Rochon, Stephen. Author interview, June 18, 1998, Baltimore, MD.

———. "Memorandum to Commandant, re: Gold Lifesaving Award Recommendation for the Crew of the Pea Island Lifesaving Station." May 9, 1995, Baltimore, MD.

Rochon, Stephen, and Kruska, Ed. "The Pea Island Legacy." *Coast Guard Reservist* (October 1996): 4–7.

Wright, David and Zoby, David. "The Pea Island Lifesavers: Black Surfmen Remembered." *Coastwatch* (May/June 1995): 3–9.

———. "Ignoring Jim Crow: The Turbulent Appointment of Richard Etheridge and the Pea Island Lifesavers." *Journal of Negro History* (March 1995): 65–80.

Zoby, David. Author interview (via phone), August 1998.

Katie Burkart Collection (KBC)

Harper's Weekly (HW)

National Park Service (NPS)

North Carolina Aquarium on Roanoke Island (NCA)

North Carolina Collection, University of North
    Carolina–Chapel Hill Library (UNC)

North Carolina Division of Archives and History
    (NCDAH)

Outer Banks History Center (OBHC)

U.S. Coast Guard (USCG)

R. E. Griffith, artist, U.S. Fish and Wildlife Service
    (USFWS)

SOURCES

Cover: James Melvin, artist

Introduction: UNC

Chapter 1: Harper's Weekly (1862); UNC; *Animate Creation,* vol. 2 (1885); Carole Weatherford, artist; UNC.

Chapter 2: UNC; NCDAH; UNC; UNC; Massachusetts Commandery, Military Order of the Loyal Legion and the U.S. Army Military History Institute.

Chapter 3: UNC.

Chapter 4: UNC; UNC; *The National Cyclopedia of American Biography;* OBHC; *Harper's Weekly* (1888); USCG; *Annual Report of the Operations of the U.S. Lifesaving Service* (1900); NPS; USCG; USCG; USCG; OBHC; UNC; NPS; OBHC; *Harper's Weekly* (1853).

Chapter 5: NCDAH; *Harper's Weekly* (1888); *Harper's Weekly* (1888); *Harper's Weekly* (1888); USFWS; USFWS.

Chapter 6: USFWS; OBHC.

Chapter 7: NCDAH; National Archives, East Point, Georgia; USFWS; KBC; NCA; OBHC; USCG; USCG.

Chapter 8: USCG; USCG; USCG; USCG; USCG (official photo); KBC; KBC.

Chapter 9: USCG; USCG; NCA.

Carole Boston Weatherford is the author of several books for young people, including *Grandma and Me; Mighty Menfolk; Me and the Family Tree;* and *Juneteenth Jamboree.* She also authored *The Tan Chanteuse,* a prize-winning poetry chapbook. Among her many honors are a North Carolina Arts Council Writers Fellowship, the North Carolina Poetry Society Caldwell Nixon Award, a North Carolina Press Association Award and the Furious Flower Poetry Prize. She lives with her family in High Point, North Carolina.